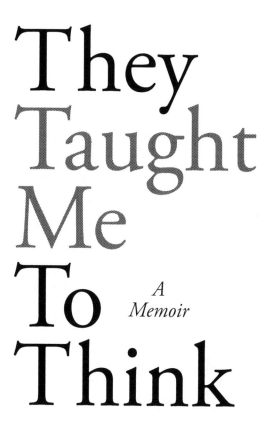

They Taught Me To Think

A Memoir

Michelle A. Edwards

WESTBOW
P R E S S®
A DIVISION OF THOMAS NELSON
& ZONDERVAN

Scripture quotations marked MSG are taken from THE MESSAGE, copyright © 1993, 1994, 1995, 1996, 2000, 2001, 2002 by Eugene H. Peterson. Used by permission of NavPress. All rights reserved. Represented by Tyndale House Publishers, Inc.

Scripture quotations marked (NIV) are taken from the Holy Bible, New International Version®, NIV®. Copyright © 1973, 1978, 1984, 2011 by Biblica, Inc.™ Used by permission of Zondervan. All rights reserved worldwide. www.zondervan.com The "NIV" and "New International Version" are trademarks registered in the United States Patent and Trademark Office by Biblica, Inc.™

This book is a work of non-fiction. Unless otherwise noted, the author and the publisher make no explicit guarantees as to the accuracy of the information contained in this book and in some cases, names of people and places have been altered to protect their privacy.

WestBow Press books may be ordered through booksellers or by contacting:

WestBow Press
A Division of Thomas Nelson & Zondervan
1663 Liberty Drive
Bloomington, IN 47403
www.westbowpress.com
1 (866) 928-1240

Because of the dynamic nature of the Internet, any web addresses or links contained in this book may have changed since publication and may no longer be valid. The views expressed in this work are solely those of the author and do not necessarily reflect the views of the publisher, and the publisher hereby disclaims any responsibility for them.

Any people depicted in stock imagery provided by Thinkstock are models, and such images are being used for illustrative purposes only. Certain stock imagery © Thinkstock.

ISBN: 978-1-5127-9801-2 (sc)
ISBN: 978-1-9736-1066-3 (e)

Print information available on the last page.

WestBow Press rev. date: 11/08/2017

Part One

Endorsements

Michelle rightly places creation thinking as the foundation for all of our thinking. She writes, "Through creation, God introduced a paradigm for reframing our situations: think, speak, create. To change our dark, empty, abysmal circumstances we must first see the change in our minds. We focus on the improvement, the blessing, the goal rather than on the problem or ill circumstance."

I thoroughly enjoyed Michelle's open, witty, yet sobering style of writing on how God brought her out of depression and despair to a true faith in her (our) Creator whom she dearly loves. This memoir will inspire you to believe!

Mary Ann Kaiser
Pastor and International Speaker, The Way Ministries
Author of *Love That Heals: Let My Life's Love Song Sing To You*

In *They Taught Me to Think: A Memoir,* Michelle shows a character driven by obedience, determination, and resilience. This book delivers a powerful message to all readers, particularly those who may be on the verge of doubting God's call.

Martha Joseph Watts, Ed.D
Author of *Writing to Respond to Text and Tests*

Superbly written with a rich sense of humor, *They Taught Me To Think* portrays the strength of the human spirit through a dichotomy of emotions—from despair to hope to triumph. This page-turner will leave you wanting more.

Collette Chapman
Internet Entrepreneur

Acknowledgements

Thank you to my parents, siblings, extended family, and countless friends who have been so gracious. I am better because of you.

To Dr. Martha Joseph Watts for your invaluable feedback on this book

To the faculty and staff of I.S. 347 School of Humanities in Brooklyn, New York: Your support and enthusiasm are priceless.

To the Creator who placed me in this world and at this time: I am honored to be all Yours, now and evermore.

There's no end to the publishing of books, and constant study wears you out so you're no good for anything else. The last and final word is this: Fear God. Do what he tells you.

Ecclesiastes 12:12-13, The Message

Table of Contents

Prologue

Prophecies (New York, 2003)

Prophecy 1

"These things the Lord is speaking about you: The Lord said there is this entrepreneur sitting inside of you who can take nothing and, when finished, make something out of it. God's resurrecting that part of you—that entrepreneur that's inside of you—to rise back up and get back in the battle. And I'm looking at you standing in the realm of the Spirit, and you're saying, 'If I did it for so and so, and so and so, and so and so, I can make it happen for me.'"

"It's time to rise beyond the dust of yesterday and get yourself on the frontline! There is a release upon your life in the area of entrepreneurship—something you're going to be doing with your hands that God's going to bless. It's in your hand! God will bless it. Pursue it with everything you've got because God gave it to you. And this thing you're going to do with your hand, the blessing of God is on it; the hand of the Lord is on it. It will bring you much blessing."

Prophecy 2

"This season will bring great change to you. . . . Tighten up. Tighten up areas in your life that can move you forward in the things of God. Tighten up your faith. Strengthen, strengthen, strengthen your faith."

"One more thing I hear God saying. I don't know if you are very instrumental in writing. But I see writing skills. God says, 'Write the book! Write the book. . . . You are an anointed scribe in the kingdom of God. And the printed page will speak volumes of My presence as you write. The gifting that I've given you is a creative ability to write what I'm speaking.'"

Chapter One

The Birthing of Dissonance

My mother told me the story of my birth—of her being in labor and waiting for the midwife. None of my six siblings ever gave her such trouble in childbirth. I was the one who almost took her life. She was 38 years old and pregnant in the 1960s era when women were deemed way too old to have children at that age. Her intense heart palpitations while she was in labor terrified her, and she was certain she wouldn't make it out of the delivery room alive. Every time the labor pains struck, her heart felt like it would collapse. So she used the labor pangs to push. And so it was, in one of those deep excruciating exhalations, that I arrived. My mother called for the nurse, who—upon seeing the mess on the bed—was furious that my mother had taken matters into her own hands and had pushed without supervision. But Mommy could not be bothered; she had been relieved of her pain. And I, a silent partner to her crime, remained umbilically attached yet utterly set free.

Years later when the story is retold, Mommy says that since my birth I have been impatient. I am not sure how the blame suddenly shifted to me, how it became my impatience rather than her stubbornness in not calling for the nurse sooner. And Daddy chuckles in agreement with his wife.

Of a truth, I am known for my grave impatience. But what can I say? It's the to-may-to/to-mah-to debate. My parents call it impatience; I brand it independence. However we view it, my manner of entry into this world is the context that has so shaped my existence—proactivity borne out of thirst for independence.

I surmise, too, that inherently I knew my parents had to be stopped. They already had six children, I was the seventh, and there were no plans to discontinue this baby-making trend. But enough was enough! They had followed well God's directive to multiply and replenish the earth. It was time for them to retire from childbearing. So as my first act of altruism, I had entered this world with a heightened—perhaps even divine—sense of social equity to level the reproductive playing field and end my parents' apparent quest to abuse God's gift of childbearing.

Chapter Two

Meet the Family

I was born and raised in Guyana, on the northern tip of South America. The only English-speaking country in the continent, Guyana was a colony of the Dutch and later of the Brits until independence in 1966. I was born a year after we obtained independence from England, so I didn't experience the colonial lifestyle. Whatever glimpses I get of those days are from reading and from the stories of my parents and my older siblings.

My parents are from the countryside, villages apart. My father and his three now-deceased siblings are the products of a hard-working farmer and his equally industrious wife. Mommy grew up on a sugar plantation. Her mother was a homemaker, and my maternal grandfather was an irrigation laborer in the sugar estate. Though my parents had very few material goods, they treasured education. So, from the age of sixteen, Mommy worked as a teacher, later advancing to the position of head-teacher. Daddy worked his way up to being chief public health inspector. With strong work ethics and a commitment to self-empowerment, my parents built a family of good repute. Ours was a typical middle-class family in Guyana. We seven children were held together by parents who balanced well professionalism on the job and personal leadership at home. My childhood was filled with fun sports, particularly cricket and athletics; indoor games; and family gatherings. Our family of nine, including our parents, was more than enough, so there was little need to solicit friends to join us. The Edwards family was its own mishmash of players, scorers, hecklers, and cheerleaders.

Most weekends after chores had been completed one could expect a robust game of saul pass or cricket to be launched in the driveway. The game organizer was usually Greg, firstborn and sportsman extraordinaire. (I say sportsman extraordinaire, as he would later earn a spot as wicketkeeper-batsman on Guyana's national cricket team.)

Saul pass was played by marking the ground with chalk to create boxes. Each of the two teams took turns running through or guarding the boxes. The objective was for the runners to make it through the boxes without being touched or tagged by the guards who stood at intersections within. Several runners moved through the boxes simultaneously in an effort to dodge the guards. Whoever completed the journey first won the game.

According to Greg, I was only a few months old when our sister Heather was cradling me in her arms as she stood on the driveway watching a spirited game of saul pass. Heather was reveling in the excitement of the game when Greg was ejected for unsuccessfully trying to get past a guard. Furious about his loss and equally infuriated by Heather's cackling at him, Gregory lashed out at her. The impact of his swing sent me careening out of Heather's grasp and into the putta-putta. Putta-putta was the worst kind of mud: wet, sticky, stinky, and one mini step up from feces itself. Ridding oneself of putta-putta required being hosed down outdoors as no in-house shower could adequately cleanse such filth. I was still bawling my little lungs out and waiting for deliverance from the putta-putta when Greg looked up just in time to meet Daddy's horrified gaze from the verandah. Gregory's whipping that day was inevitable.

No flogging or scolding, however, could quell the competitive spirit among the Edwards. And as we grew, so did our passion for sports and for outwitting one another.

As with any group, there are those who can and those who cannot or probably should not. My brother Roger was the latter. His six-foot-plus gait and awkward left-handedness were to blame. But Roger had a mean swing and a reach for saul pass. His sinistral edge worked well in that it caught runners off-guard, so his team usually assigned him to guard the middle row, the most difficult section for runners to get through. Towering over the rest of the players, Roger was a silent menace. While others laughed and taunted one another, Roger didn't say much. He glared, then averted his gaze as he paced his turf. That was his opponents' warning to not even think of getting past him. Roger never just tagged the losers with the requisite tap on the torso. Instead, he arched his long body every which way to extend as far into the runner's lane as he could. The unlucky victim who trespassed into his reach was slapped with enough ferocity to put him or her out of commission for the rest of the game. Roger's glee was his primary reward.

The only person slick enough to escape Roger's defense was Kevin. Kevin was as adept in sports as he was in mischief. It was he who provoked our retriever Bruno by offering food and constantly pulling it away before the dog could get at it. So often Kevin entertained himself by terrorizing the poor animal. It was only a matter of time before Bruno toppled him and put an end to the abuse.

It was this same Kevin who swapped lime rickey for karela (bitter melon/gourd) juice and set it in the fridge for Greg. Hot and thirsty from a day hanging out with his friends, Greg returned home and bolted for the fridge. On seeing the appetizingly cold drink, he guzzled the beverage only to realize midstream—to the sheer amusement of the rest of us—its pungent, bitter finish.

And, thanks to Kevin, how often had Mommy fumed in exasperation upon finding that her freshly baked cake had collapsed. For years she blamed herself, her methods, the ingredients. Should we have told her it was that twerp who purposely opened and closed the oven door before the cake had set—all because he liked the texture and taste of fallen cake over perfectly risen cake? It was always Kevin with the mischief, and no one was safe. Even years later in young adulthood, when my life seemed to be going nowhere, it was Kevin again who jested to our parents that they were better off "investing in cattle" than in raising Michelle.

To round off the Edwards clan were Dillon and Diane. Dillon was the good son, an easygoing lad whose days were split between helping Mommy in the kitchen and driving his imaginary car in the yard. Two years younger than Dillon and a year older than I, Diane was our resident prim and proper lady. She and I were joined at the hip because of age and gender. We, too, were included in the sports, but it was always a risk to have Diane on one's team. Heaven forbid that the cricket ball, for instance, be hit in her direction and end up in a puddle. This signaled a virtual pause in play for Diane as she could not, would not, soil her hands—not in a pond, not near a frond; not o'er a wall, not for a ball. It didn't matter that her team mates screamed furiously at her. Diane tiptoed around the tall grass, making sure not to step on anything objectionable. And as she took cursory inventory of the site, her hands splayed in detestation, the batsman continued to score.

In a dash, I would whiz past Diane and plough through the razor grass, oblivious to the sharp edges that cut worse than paper nicks. Parting the grass frantically, I would find the ball and hurl it to the wicketkeeper before another run was made. Diane, meanwhile, would return to her safe spot on the edge of the driveway completely unfazed.

The game was never that serious for our lady, Di.

Chapter Three

They Taught Me To Think

Change is inevitable, and over time the dynamics of our family shifted. My family immigrated to New York in search of the American dream. In this proverbial First World paradise, my parents traded their lifestyle in the Tropics for implicit indentureship. Having enjoyed the privileges of being a high-level educator in Guyana, my mother, in her fifties, worked as a nanny in New York. And my father, a previously prominent public servant in his native government, could find employment only as a security guard.

The promise of a better life in America propelled my parents towards such sacrifice on behalf of their adult children. Education was the route one commonly traveled to this destination. So it was this commute to academic enlightenment that my sister Diane and I, the two youngest in the family, were instructed to take. Our other siblings were expected to find full-time work to sustain the family.

By the time we had spent five years in the USA, most of my siblings had married and had their own

American-born children. My brother Dillon and I were the only siblings living at home in New York with our parents. Our married siblings lived elsewhere in New York and in Georgia. Then, after completing undergraduate and graduate degrees in New York and teaching English for a few years, I accepted an editorial job in Springfield, Missouri. I was happy to bid farewell to the pervasive bustle of the Big Apple.

It was while living in the Midwest that I heard several times the statement that would probe my mind indefinitely: "My father/mother taught me to think." In every instance, the speaker was a female acquaintance of mine who attributed this praise to one or the other of her parents. I was mesmerized by these declarations as I had never heard the phrase *taught me to think* nor had the most obvious fact that thinking is learned behavior even occurred to me. The resonance of this new-to-me phrase prompted my own cognitive scrutiny.

On a subliminal level, I could rationalize that thinking is taught; else, how would one explain socialization? But teaching to think and teaching how to think are dissimilar. The former assumes independence, where the teacher creates the environment for the learner to explore, challenge, discuss, and debate. The latter connotes subjugation and dependence, where the learner's point of view mirrors that of the teacher.

At this point of my personal inquiry, I had lived more than three decades. Although a postgraduate student, I felt swindled out of something fundamental, something these Mid-western women had—a legacy of independent thinking. I thought of my own cognitive heritage and quickly realized mine was a pedigree that did not celebrate independent thought or self-expression. Rather, my inherited socio-academic curriculum espoused that compliance was key to success. In such an environment, rote learning and uncontested obedience were lauded. Deviation from that norm earned no rewards. For adults in this culture, success often meant transferring their mores to children and reveling in the continuation of their legacy—a legacy in which adults were always right and could not be challenged by youth.

Somewhere between pursuing the dream and my newfound introspection on cognition, I considered the entrapment of being in a cultural dichotomy where younger immigrants contended with the dissonance of living through our parents' worldview or adopting that of the new world. We were our parents' children. They had birthed, nurtured, and invested in us. We owed them loyalty and respect. And while we adult children had assimilated into the US, our parents were often still adjusting to the foreign culture yet trying to maintain control of the family. They were struggling with odd norms such as American teenagers leaving home at eighteen years old to find their places in the world. For us, children didn't live away from the family home except when married or, in extreme cases, when taking a job far away. Single sons and daughters lived with their parents until one or the other died. That was an integral part of our birthright. In this adopted land of America, we were expected to honor our parents in this and other ways.

We should do as they and their fore-parents had done. We should think as they did. The geography of living in a foreign country with foreign rules did not alter that expectation.

At the same time, we adult children were products of our new world, having lived and been educated in America for some time. The theories of higher education had taught us to ask deeper questions and challenge norms. We had learned that no authority figure—parental, parochial, political, or else—was exempt from scrutiny or challenge. Our exposure to higher-level thinking, by virtue of our parents' own intent and ambitions, had introduced a whole new way of thinking about the parent/adult-child relationship.

Chapter Four

Failing and Flailing

Early in 2011, I relocated from Missouri to Atlanta, Georgia, to assist my brother Greg with the care of our then-octogenarian parents. Our parents had moved residence to Georgia after the sudden death of Dillon, who had been their caregiver in New York. I was honored to serve my geezers by joining hands with Greg. Our parents were (and are) great people who had done so much for us children, and it was our time to be there for them.

I had saved enough money to sustain me for a few months, so I rented a place near my parents and set about applying for work. Daily I applied for jobs but with no positive outcome. After four months of the routine, I grew tired of filling out applications, entering the same biographical data every time. I was tired of tweaking my resume and cover letter to match jobs. *What was the deal?* Surely, I was qualified and skilled to work in my field, but somehow nothing opened up. I applied for editing jobs, teaching positions, office gigs. I targeted employers, recruiters, friends, family. When months went by without tangible results, my hope plummeted. I retreated into silence, depression, darkness. In those days, I refused to talk to God, for there was nothing more to say to Him. Taking my petition to Him seemed fruitless. I was hurt, abandoned, and alone. Our relationship had hit a grainy patch, though deep within I knew I could never leave Him. Where would I go? I couldn't live without God. And I knew He would never leave me. Still the loneliness was unbearable.

My days were spent balancing my job search with finding clients for the home-based copy-editing services I resurrected. I was panicking much as the editing projects I got were sketchy, and my savings were dwindling rapidly. I needed to find reliable income. Eventually, through one of Greg's contacts, I landed a part-time job at a local college.

In the freshman writing class I was teaching there, I asked the students to write a descriptive essay about anyone in the room. One student who chose me as his subject penned: "She is always well-dressed, which tells me that she must be getting paid a pretty good amount of money." If only that boy knew how underpaid and unraveled I really was. Whatever fashion he thought I sported those days had been acquired from my life before Atlanta. The truth was that the part-time earnings from the college job weren't enough to sustain me. I was flailing and failing miserably. Yes, I had a solid education, years of professional experience, good family and friends. But I was broke and broken. I was embarrassingly underemployed and underpaid, and playing dodge ball with bill collectors had become tedious. So when my countless efforts to find full-time employment were denied for two consecutive years, depression returned.

I lost hope. The system had played me, for I had bought into the illusion that higher education equaled more money and carte blanche to the American dream. I realized then that a college education no longer offered guarantee of employment. The rules of the game had changed, but I evidently never got an update.

During that time of depression, I slept a lot during the day and night. At night, I welcomed sleep, for it suspended my despair. Most of my time at home was spent in bed and in my dark apartment, where I kept the lights off (except for a night-light) and the curtains closed.

A by-product of enduring such hardship is that it strips not just you but also those close to you. It shows who you are and reveals the character of your inner circle. It exposes those who are for you and those against you. It purges, probably like no other purgative. I recall a conversation with a relative who could not fathom my fate.

> "Michelle," she piped. "Wha' happened to you? You had so much promise. I don't understand why you struggling like this."

She didn't intend the accusatory tone. She was as confused as I and trying to be empathetic. But the question was not necessary. Did she not think I had those same queries about my present and future states? My life had become sad, pathetic. There I was, a dissertation shy of a doctorate degree yet could not find full-time work. I had lost my will to dream, to think, to hope, to create, to change my circumstance. I had become a joke among my family and close friends—an example of what not to do, what not to be.

Somewhere in those depressing moments, I remembered words God had spoken to me almost a decade before. I recalled His affirmation of my talents and value. I heard again the instruction He had given me through the mouths of several contemporary visionaries: "Write the book." I heard this particular directive so often that it haunted me. The command was never to write *a* book, for that I probably could do easily. The edict was to write *the* book. That specificity haunted me, for I felt I had to get it right. *What book, God?* Surely, I had a story to tell, but there was so much . . . some of which I was hesitant to reveal.

I grappled with the age-old conundrum of why the righteous suffer. While I still cannot resolve this mystery, I did suspect my misery was a result of unbelief and disobedience. I had circumvented God's mandate for my life and cowardly settled for the status quo. I knew I should have been working on the book, but I was afraid to be known in my family as "the writer." In a general sense, that title carried its own stigma of idleness, pretense, poverty. Presenting that career choice to the Edwards clan would have meant professional suicide and a lifetime of mockery. I still remembered when, in my late teens, I switched college majors from biology to English and heavy hitters in the family berated me.

"Who goes to college for four years to
study English? You know English already.
You just lazy, Michelle, you lazy!"

I was too inexperienced then to openly challenge the
naysayers. In their world, studying the arts and humanities
was useless. What mattered to them was pursuing careers
in law, medicine, or the like. Of course, in reality none of
these naysayers was a lawyer, doctor, or the like. But that
was a typical paradox.

I had long discovered a natural propensity for writing,
however, and wanted to hone it. So, desperate for change
out of the Georgia despair, I set about rediscovering my
will to fight—the same will that had propelled my birth
out of the constraints of nature's womb and had delivered
me into the world. What had caused such unfettering?
Was it something innate about that baby? Was it external,
in the environment that had surrounded her? Whatever
it was, little baby Michelle had defied those constraints.
She had been eager, excited, relentless, determined, and
unrestrained to initiate her salvation in an unconventional
way. And decades after her dramatic physical birth, she
would initiate her exit from gloom and burst into the
light.

Chapter Five

Think, Speak, Create

Laughter has a special way of brightening my perspective, and comedic television shows play their role here. In the days of darkness in Georgia, I depended heavily on my comic favorites to make me smile. And they didn't fail. From the quirkiness of Mr. Bean to the narcissism/borderline lunacy of Hyacinth Bucket and the numerous American sitcoms in syndication—*Friends, Frasier, The Fresh Prince of Bel-Air*. The daftness of Rose juxtaposed with the slick wit of Sophia in *The Golden Girls*; everything *Seinfeld*; the dimwittedness of Mayor Winston in *Spin City*; the chronic abuse of Deborah and Robert in *Everybody Loves Raymond*; the dramatic vocal intonations of the late Phil Hartman in *NewsRadio*; and the candor that always backfired on Larry David in *Curb Your Enthusiasm*. I gorged on these shows, admiring the craft and imagining what it must be like on those writing teams. The energy, the ideas, the follies, the brilliance of it all! These laugh agents allowed me to suspend my dismal existence if only for a moment. But the relief was artificial, short-lived. I would no sooner be forced to return to reality.

During those days I was introduced to the life coaching of prominent motivational teachers who confirmed that if we don't plan our lives others will do so for us. The implication was that each person was responsible to create, envision, and plan the life he or she wanted. Failure to do such diligence made one easy prey to others' whims and fancies. Therefore, we should consider our natural gifts and talents and think carefully of ways to reinvent and reinvest them. Our existence was not for self-aggrandizement but rather for fulfilling God's purposes by using the treasures He deposited in us—treasures that improved our world and poised us for eternal paradise.

I studied again the biblical record of creationism, where "earth was a soup of nothingness, a bottomless emptiness, an inky blackness" (Genesis 1:1, MSG). Then, I noticed the pattern. God, our Creator, had modeled the creative process. He demonstrated how to change circumstances. Faced with an existence of lack, absence, emptiness, etc., God himself decided to change those conditions. His method? Thinking, speaking, creating. Into the abyss of nothingness, God envisioned life with all its expansive, diverse, complicated trappings: the sky, heavens, earth, land, oceans, galaxies, air, plants, animals, humans, and everything between. God thought it all first; then, He spoke it into being; and the universe was created. Things great and small were materialized. Things that pleased Him. Things He admired. Things He blessed. Then, God rested.

Through creation, God introduced a paradigm for reframing our situations: think, speak, create. To change our dark, empty, abysmal circumstances, we must first see the change in our minds. We focus on the improvement, the blessing, the goal rather than on the problem or ill circumstance. Empowered with this perspective, we speak life into the abysses to change their outcomes. Such thinking is a necessary precursor to success. Without vision, nothing of value can be created. Everything we experience—every comfort, convenience, invention, sophistication, etc.—is a result of countless thinkers and visionaries creating life through their thoughts and following through with tangible plans and actions.

In becoming adult and following the course of traditional education, I had long forgotten how to think in this way, how to dream and have vision. I had traded my youthful, creative reservoir for the exhausting boredom and predictability of adult normalcy. In living the status quo, every normal route I took ended in a pitfall of despair and dissatisfaction. Now I was relearning how to be childlike. I was learning how to think in ways that changed outcomes and produced results. The battle had always been in the mind. I was reframing my mind and creating a world of positives and possibilities. I understood the importance of mind protection as I meditated on the apostle Paul's advice to fill our minds with things that are "true, noble, reputable, authentic, compelling, gracious—the best, not the worst; the beautiful, not the ugly; things to praise, not things to curse" (Philippians 4:8, MSG).

Applying these principles, I thought actively of the

quality of life I desired: where and how I wanted to live, what professional and personal goals I wanted to accomplish, what impact I wanted to make in society and in the kingdom of God. It had been ages since I thought of such things. How invigorating to project into the future! The light had finally broken through.

The first night of this enlightenment, I hardly slept. I had been aroused by sheer excitement, anticipation, and the barely familiar feeling of hope and possibility. The dream had begun to take shape, and I was too exhilarated to rest. Sleep would be a deterrent to my accomplishments. I had lost so much time in darkness and depression, and now my eyes were adjusting remarkably to the new light. The laptop became my pillow as I wrote and napped, soaking in every exciting moment of this personal revival.

In that time of dream creation and vision casting, I realized how much I wanted to live on the Florida coast. The easy access to expanses of ocean and waterways was tantalizing. I fantasized of lingering on the edge of the shore with my feet pressed comfortably into the sand. I could feel the warm grains filling the crevices between my toes. I remembered my youth when Daddy took Diane and me to the ocean shore. We waited excitedly for the waves to come up and wash the sand from our bare feet. Then, we'd outrun the ocean water to a particular place on the shore. Sometimes we won. Other times the waves came in too fast and hard, and our legs could not power through them to the imaginary finish line on shore. That's how we non-swimmers engaged with the ocean in the old country; we raced against the waves. I missed those days. I missed that access to nature. I longed for the ocean's playfulness and indulgence. I wanted all of that again on a regular basis—the adult version of childhood.

But the guilt of leaving my parents paralyzed me. I had moved to Georgia to be there for them, to serve them, and to help Greg. How could I jump ship because things got rough? Then, in one of our father-daughter bonding sessions en route to the market, Daddy came to my rescue. I proposed to him my wish to relocate to Florida. I sought his permission to expand the job search, explaining my great desire for the Sunshine State and admitting guilt with thinking of leaving him and Mommy. Daddy stopped short of scolding me. He had seen firsthand the suffering I was enduring in Georgia and insisted that I needed to make a life for myself wherever I chose.

Less than one month later, I was called for an interview in Florida and landed the job. To say I was ecstatic is an obvious understatement. Things were turning around in my favor.

Chapter Six

The Dying of Dissonance

Lathering up in the shower one morning, I felt a lump on my left breast. It had appeared suddenly, obtrusively. At first, I thought what any woman faced with such discovery would think. And just as quickly I dismissed the thought. I had no health insurance, so there lay my temporary justification for denial. But two menstrual cycles later when the lump had become more pronounced, dimpled, and tingly, I conceded that there was no recourse.

I was forced to address this most inconvenient anomaly. I was certain by then that I wasn't ready to give up and die—not that anything was wrong with that, for death is inevitable. In fact, I actually anticipated the euphoria of heaven, of sitting in perpetual bliss with the One who created, sustained, and loved me. I thought of the amazing biblical records of heaven—that perfectly designed city of resplendent walls and gates of pearls. God's golden metropolis translucent as glass and built with every precious gem imaginable. The ultimate real estate paradise wherein the presence of sun or moon is simply redundant, as God himself is the light. Who could fathom such unparalleled splendor? Who would resist that opulence?

Nothing on earth could outdo this promise of eternal bliss with my King and Lord. Nothing could possibly compare to this magnificent Wonder of the Universe. I had embraced the apostle Paul's affirmation that to be absent from the body is to be present with the Lord. What better offer could there ever be! How awesome would it be finally to see my majestic, eternal, sovereign King face to face. I couldn't think of a better prize. But, alas, there were specific tasks to complete on earth, and I should not return to my heavenly Father with an "Incomplete" grade. I had to make Him proud by finishing my assignment here.

I recalled the many testimonies of women who survived breast cancer—extraordinary, everyday women, popular celebrities, plus millions of other survivors globally. I was encouraged by the advances in medical technology that facilitated a good quality of life for survivors. If that lump meant what I thought it could mean, I would fight and win.

Persistent searching led me to a low-cost, local clinic from where I was referred to a medical center for a mammogram. The mammogram and ultrasound revealed irregularities that warranted a biopsy. I smiled internally at the doctor's post-ultrasound assessment: "Ms. Edwards, there is a suspicious lump on your breast. . . ." Sarcasm got the better of me as I mused, "Really, dude? Are you always this good at stating the obvious?" Of course, there was a suspicious lump on my breast! Why else was I there? Why else was I contorting around the mammogram machine in postures that would make ballerinas wince? Why else would I offer up my body to be so manhandled?

I stopped myself. This was no time to be sassy. I should put out good thoughts, good vibes for a good outcome. But maybe the damage in my wayward thinking was already done, for one week later I received the biopsy results: cancer of the left breast and left axillary lymph nodes.

Fear nabbed me as I wrestled with the ambivalence of giving up or fighting. I thought deeply about the fact that I had accomplished so little. I had so much more to give and do yet hadn't even managed to show the world my gift, my potential, my true self. I had been living in the shadows of familial expectations yet so desperately wanted to present myself to the world and to the God above. A non-verbal yet audible, "Tada! I'm here. I'm here to do my part." But I hadn't done my part. I was here but had not yet showcased my talent and labor in a way that distinguished me and that expressed my particular appreciation for having been blessed with life.

The news of the diagnosis left me afraid, frustrated, and tired. I was tired of suffering. First, the three years of grave underemployment and hardship in Georgia and all the stress that built from that. Then, just when things were turning around for me and I had finally been hired in the locale of my dreams, I received this dreadful diagnosis. The pity party I hosted was nothing spectacular—only the usual guests: my pillow and me in my darkened bedroom. A lone nightlight in the bathroom offered illumination for my frequent toilet trips. Neither my dearest Mr. Bean nor Hyacinth Bucket, aka Bouquet, could penetrate the despair of those days. I was fed up. I was fed up with life and fed up with suffering. When would I have a break? Everyone in my life knew that "Michelle don't multitask," so the idea of managing such big things simultaneously was nerve-racking. The thought of relocating to my dream state for a new job while dealing with breast cancer and all that came with it irritated me. A dreadful inconvenience this was! Why couldn't I just have the joy of celebrating Florida and all that it represented? Had I not suffered enough? The pity party was in full swing when my friend Marcia called and spoke the following words to me: "Girl, God obviously has a lot of faith in your ability to manage this situation. Maybe He chose you to go through this because He knows you can handle it."

The morbid party noise in my head halted. I was silenced, relieved, invigorated. What a perspective! Marcia's words triggered the recollection of biblical Job, a great man whom God allowed to be brutally tested by the devil. Of course, I had no business comparing myself to Job, but he was my only frame of reference in that moment.

After a few days of thinking, praying, and listening to God, I embraced the notion that God trusted me to handle this test. The devil was putting me through the wringer, an arrangement God must have permitted. So if God had such confidence in me, if He was indeed boasting about His girl Michelle, then why not engage in the showdown?

How spoiled and selfish we humans are! We are constantly in the habit of asking God to do for us, incessantly begging and bombarding Him for our own needs and desires. How about we do something for Him once in a while? How about we give Him opportunities to brag about us? How about we prove our love for Him by sacrificing our wills, our comforts, our goals, our desires, our lives? Does He not deserve such devotion? Is He not worthy of our time—the time He lent us—in this way?

Enduring this trial would be part of my devotion to God. I would be strong and honor Him. Even in those moments when my flesh fails, I will still honor God, for He is my strength, my hope, my salvation, my rock, my love. I love Him now and always. I will never leave or forsake Him. There shall be no compromise, no negotiations around this love. That's just the way it is, the way it ever will be. And if I perish in the passion of such love, so be it. I will have died for a great cause.

Chapter Seven

Dream State

Energized by the prospect of a new life, I set my sights towards Florida. Before I relocated from Georgia, the Lord provided the means for me to have a lumpectomy through the state's medical funding. Some members of the family were very concerned about my leaving Georgia, where there was ample family support to help me manage recovery. My sister Heather advised that maybe moving to a new state where there was little family support plus starting a new job were probably not the best things to do right then. But I had little to no recourse. There was nothing left for me in Georgia. I had given the Peach State three years of my life, and mostly misery had come of it. It was time to move on and live my dream. If cancer would take me out of this world, it would have to fight me in Florida. I would not cower. I would not go gentle into that good night. I would fight for my life and for my dream.

I was and still am a child of the King; it was His report that I believed. I never did embrace breast cancer in my body. From the inception I viewed it as an anomaly, a foreign thing that had no business being in me. In each visit with doctors, nurses, etc., I reiterated my position that the thing was an abnormality. Surely, this was obvious, but I intentionally spoke life to my body and to the surrounding atmosphere. I was thinking, speaking, and creating life just like my Creator taught. This disease did not belong in my family, and it certainly was illegal in me. What kind of a faithless coward would I then be to allow the unlawful to deter me from my future?

So off I went to the state of my dreams, having accepted a position teaching English at a public high school in Florida. I had taught college students in New York and Atlanta, so high school teaching would be a cinch. And how good it felt to be accepted for a full-time position after years of rejection and frustration in Atlanta.

I chose Florida because it was my place of paradise. I wanted the coastal warmth and unlimited access to Caribbean culture and food. I wanted to walk barefoot in the yard most of the year and flounce in sundresses in the fall. I wanted to be Floridian—to call the Sunshine State home. And though high school teaching was not the ideal, the job did get me to my dream state.

I was assigned to teach 10th and 12th graders. Within the first week, I realized how unprepared I was for teaching at the high school level. From constantly yelling at disruptive students, to monitoring others so they conformed to the litany of school-imposed rules, to spoon-feeding and listening to their constant pleas for validation—it was beyond exhausting.

Less than one month into the gig, I came to terms with my absolute disdain of the job. It was an unrelenting grind from which neither evenings nor weekends offered reprieve. Time not spent in the classroom was spent creating lesson plans, writing reports, grading, responding to email, and attending meetings. The ongoing onslaught of to-dos promised no end in sight. Day after day, I muttered in exasperation, "Too much; it's just too much." I thought maybe it was my maladjustment to the public high school environment, but even seasoned teachers were suffering. Daily they, too, dragged their limp bodies up staircases and through the halls, their faces drained, their wills visibly compromised. How relieved I was on seeing this, for it meant I was not the only one flailing.

To compound this unremitting drudgery was the students' lack of respect for authority. Never before had I experienced blatant insults and abuse from students. My most brutal shocker came a few weeks into the term when I reprimanded a student for her incessant talking during class. After warning her repeatedly to stop, I finally ousted her from the class. Without missing a beat, she popped out of her seat in profaned revolt.

I was too stunned to respond verbally. I simply stared at her and held the gaze until she exited the class. It was all the strength I could muster to avoid appearing weak. That was the first day I cried in class. Not in front of the students, of course. But after class ended, I quietly and pensively dried my tears. Was this what my life had come to? Tolerating insolence from slackers who couldn't distinguish a noun from a verb? I was appalled that a student would even think of speaking to a teacher that way.

I cried because of the disrespect and because of my inability to manage the hooliganism. And had I even hinted at insulting a student in such a way, I would have made national news. Yet these students got away with all sorts of atrocities, and there was little the teacher could do.

I cringed every day and cried a lot. I dreaded waking in the morning and going to work, but the memory of previous underemployment kept me from quitting. I counted the hours at work, longing to get through the first three periods so I could break for lunch. Lunch, for me, was not a meal. It was a moment to exhale. I was so unnerved that I could not eat. With each passing day my stomach became queasier. If I ate or drank anything, I ran the risk of having diarrhea. Call it mind over matter or whatever else. The fact is that I could not take the chance of compromising classroom time by sitting on a toilet at work. So for months I ate nothing before or during school time. My only meals were at dinner and on weekends.

At the end of each school day, I could barely wait to lock the classroom door and bolt from the premises. I was becoming *that* worker—the sort who did the minimum and stayed only for a paycheck. I didn't like it. I needed out!

It was clear to me that my happiness would be had not through the security of a traditional paycheck but only by doing what I loved to do, what I was wired to do—write and edit full-time. That was my dream job. It was all I had ever wanted to do but was always too afraid to embrace. How unexpected that such fear be so swiftly assuaged at the hands of hooligans.

Chapter Eight

Apprehending the Dream

Ephesians 4 was the textual reference one Sunday morning when Pastor shared his desire for us as a church to emerge in our gifts. Those words resounded in me. I needed to emerge, to break out, to be my best self with the gift God had put in my hands. The teaching job did not allow me such fulfillment. Thus, I would rise in faith again and trust God for another opportunity to do what I felt gifted to do. I was getting tired of asking God for things when He had already given so much. But my situation at the high school was not working. So I implored my heavenly Father once again.

I needed to fulfill God's intent for my life, and that was to write and edit professionally. When in my youth I had envisioned my life, I saw myself working from home. Back then, the vision was of me living in a ranch-styled house in the countryside and writing from my office at home. I never understood the lone horse in the backyard. He must have been left behind by the house's previous owners because there was and is nothing in me that finds horse-riding or rearing appealing.

In more recent vision casting, I released the horse, and my relationship with my bed became increasingly obsessive. I simply loathed leaving it. Some writers use a desk, library, coffee-house, etc. My creative space was my bed, surrounded by minimal light, an overhead fan, and no less than 70 degrees temperature. There was nothing spectacular about my wooden, queen-sized bed. In fact, it was not even *my* bed, but rather the bed that came with the manufactured house I was renting in Florida. The pillows and linens were mine, my meager attempt to claim some semblance of ownership. Next to me on the bedside table was often the residue of some beverage. I drank more than ate, as eating required too much food preparation and time consumption.

It was time to revamp my website and throw my energies into building my brand. A quick email to my tech guy set things in motion. We would start redesigning my website the following day; the teaching job would be the conduit to needed finances. It was the middle of November 2014, and I had less than two months to become financially fluid so I wouldn't have to teach. The end of 2014 was my deadline. I had absolutely no desire to return to teaching high school in spring 2015. I couldn't even imagine what that would entail. Somehow I had to write and market insatiably. There was no way I could pull this off in such short time, except through the God who annihilates impossibilities.

I was so excited to be dreaming again, to have projections for my life and future. I didn't take that privilege for granted. I knew how dark and futile life was without the ability to see a good future. The absence of such vision is sure death. Therefore, I would be intentional about living to the fullest. I would live abundantly, and my dreams would propel me. My vision, in addition to writing, editing, and publishing, was to own a four-bedroom, Mediterranean-styled house with enough room for a cellar and a hammock. The hammock was a necessity. I had mused about having a helper, telling my friends of my intent to acquire a hammock and a helpmate who would cater to my culinary needs. The hammock was attainable; the mate, less feasible.

I preferred one from Guyana—a hammock, that is—but would settle for a locally crafted one in the meantime. The hammock would be my bed away from bed, wherein I would eat, sleep, read, write, and pray. I'd mount it on my back porch and recline daily. This venue of respite and peace would be conducive to the kind of output I needed to deliver. God had given me a mulligan of sorts, and I would maximize it well.

Meanwhile at the high school, my principal saw how much I failed at the job. His pep-talks and visits to my class decreased while our hallway greetings became obligatory. He was a decent man and a strong teacher advocate, but it was only a matter of time before one of us did that which was necessary. So I initiated the dialogue.

> "Sir, we both know that this is not working. Not for me, not for the students, not for the institution."

He agreed and had been planning to put me out of my misery even before I spoke with him. My last day of employment was the end of term on December 19, 2014.

The morning after my termination from the high school, I was at the car dealership waiting for an oil change. Freedom from the repressive teaching workload was incredible. I could not recall when last I had felt so liberated. This would be the beginning of many weekends without papers to grade, lessons to plan, reports to generate, data to process, email to manage, and mind-numbing meetings to anticipate. There would be no more temporary weekend exhalations until the cringe-inducing Monday through Friday torture. I had my life back and almost didn't know how to behave.

For starters, there were more than enough neglected house chores to catch up on, but beyond those my life now consisted of writing and building my brand. Oh, the joy! I could hardly believe I had allowed fear to derail me from this quest for so many years. And while I couldn't anticipate the date or amount of my next paycheck, faith required that I trust God to handle that. He had prompted this career change; therefore, it was His responsibility to take care of my necessities. I knew unreservedly that the resources would come as I believed and obeyed by faith. For if disobedience had brought me so much distress, then surely obedience to God would have a counter effect.

At the dawn of 2015, I determined even more to live God's way, to burn my contingencies and obey God. This meant committing to finishing the long-overdue book. It was time to abandon the cowardice that had strangled me. Almost instantly, I felt the lightness of walking in God's will. The morning of (what would have been for me) the first day of school for spring 2015, I rolled out of bed and shuffled towards the kitchen for a glass of water. I looked up at the clock sleepily and smiled. It was a few minutes before 8:00. This was my new life; I would bask in the freedom.

I needed to formulate a schedule to stay on course with my goals. On that particular day, my priority plans were to lounge awhile with my Lord, listen to an hour of personal development training while casually having my morning coffee, cook lunch, and write two pages of this book.

Epilogue

Thinking of Obedience

While faith in God is necessary in our efforts to please Him, faith without obedience is pointless. Obedience is doing what God says. This should not be difficult, but often our wills, egos, and fears get in the way. Nevertheless, obedience to God is paramount; without it there can be no relationship with Him, no negotiations with Him. It is futile to expect particular blessings from the hand of God when we blatantly disobey His commands. For instance, I recall those three years in Georgia when I trusted God intensely for full-time work, but nothing came of it because I had been disobedient. He had already given me a mandate to write, a mandate I had defied repeatedly. No amount of faith to believe for other things like jobs, healing, etc. could suffice until I aligned my thoughts and will with God's and did what He had instructed. It wasn't until I repented and obeyed God that things improved.

In the process of orienting ourselves to live in faith and obedience to God, we humans fail often. Yet God extends to us incredible patience, mercy, and graciousness. Though sometimes we endure suffering via our own disobedience, He spares us from so much worse. He always provides what we need. Suffering, therefore, makes us better as it brings out the best and worst in us and opens our sensibilities to God.

Righteous suffering (the kind that comes through godly obedience) aligns us closely with Jesus and the great Christian heroes whose portfolios are rife with hardships. Consider the example of Joseph who was betrayed and sold by his own brothers just because he had goals, dreams, and visions of a prosperous future. Think of Job who suffered horrendous physical ailments and loss of family and property for being a godly man. Then, there is Paul who was beheaded after having endured numerous imprisonments and abuses for proclaiming the Christ. Of course, the ultimate sufferer is Jesus Christ who was traded for a criminal and brutally murdered for crimes He did not commit. The reward is great for Christian sufferers who endure. Jesus's brother James affirms, "Anyone who meets a testing challenge head-on and manages to stick it out is mighty fortunate. For such persons loyally in love with God, the reward is life and more life" (James 1:12, MSG).

Medical Update

It is almost one year since the lumpectomy on my breast was done. Because of medical insurance snafus, I have not yet had any treatments of chemotherapy or radiation. My doctor, understandably, is losing his mind as this long period without treatment is disturbing. I have engaged a local clinic to help move the medical insurance process along. Surely, the need to follow up with an oncologist is critical in ushering the next chapter of my life.

But the God who thought, spoke, and designed all of life remains in control. None is greater than He. His timing is impeccable, and no detail escapes Him. Therefore, I wait . . . patiently, expectantly.

Part Two

Table of Contents

Endorsements

Praise for Part One

"What a great work. . . . So well written using a wonderful recipe of candor, intellectual analysis, wit, and courageous transparency."

Dr. Randy Hedlun
Dean of Graduate School, Global University, Springfield, Missouri

"Edwards showcases her wit, vulnerability, and faith in this memoir of self-discovery. This book is a delightful yet thought-provoking read that inspires you to take action and make your dreams a reality."

Katie W.
Copywriter, Jupiter, Florida

"This is nothing short of inspirational!"

Leon Whyte
Music Educator, New York

I've thrown myself headlong into your
arms—I'm celebrating your rescue.
I'm singing at the top of my lungs, I'm
so full of answered prayers.

Psalm 13:5-6, The Message

Prologue

Prophecies Continued: New York, 2003

Prophecy 1

"Michelle Edwards. ME. God says you will have more than enough. More than enough. 'This time I'll break you free from poverty, from lack, from debt. I'm testing you to see how faithful you are to Me. I've seen you worship; I've taken note of how you praise Me. Because it's not the praise of man that matters, it's that you're praising Me. And as you're praising Me, I'm praising you.'"

"This will also be a season of discovery. Discovery. You will discover more than enough in more than one area. It is also discovery of your assignment." You've been asking God, "'What is my purpose? Am I just here in church? Am I just here in the community? What is my purpose?'" God says, "'As you seek ME, you will find Me, you will find your purpose, and you'll find your destiny. The journey is not as long as it used to take, but you will go through the process that I'm bringing you through for perfection to affect the kingdom of God. . . . I have your back, and you're covered. You're covered.'"

Prophecy 2

"This is your season of new beginning. And God says you will not have to hide anymore. The purpose for hiding was so that you would not confront. But God says in this season He has given to you what you need so that you can confront those devils sent out against you. God says, 'This is your season to conquer, and this is your season of expression. . . . That which you've withheld because of rejection, it's not because I haven't given it to you, but it was fought because I gave it to you. So now as you confront it, you're gonna begin to see Me move in an unusual way. And even that which rejected you will now run to you because this is your season of expression.'"

"God says you have built up everybody else. You've been there as a support mechanism to everyone else. People that you've supported don't even look at you now. They don't even recall that you were there when they were in their beginnings. But God says, 'Don't look at that. I'm not using them to bless you. I'm sending you a new set of people that will recognize who you are in Me. And even as they come into your life, you will know them. And you will flow with them, and you will follow after them because that nugget inside of you has to come forth.' Earth is waiting on what God has placed in you."

Prophecy 3

"And I heard the voice of critics start singing your praise. 'Your critics,' the Lord says, 'will sing your praise when

I'm finished doing what I will do with you.' But the favor of God is resting on your life to bring you that which others inherited. God said, "'I will condense the years together, and in a very short time. . . . I will have achieved through you what it took others a longer time to achieve.' But this is the season to stay focused and stay on the path so that you do not miss what the Father has for you."

Chapter One

Vision

Early in the fall of 2015, I was on my way to work when my Volvo coded on Interstate 95 in Boca Raton. Vigorously praying, I chugged up the hill towards the exit. "Lord, please don't let this car die on me. Let me at least get to work on time." I trembled as irritated drivers swerved from behind. I had waited too long to land this job and wasn't about to blow it. Just two months after submitting to my publisher the manuscript for Part One of this book, I was invited to join the full-time staff of an international academic publisher in South Florida. My role as copy editor was enjoyable, the team pleasant, and the remuneration the best of my career. I would work there during the week and continue writing on weekends until my dream of successful, full-time writer was realized.

This job was important to my end game, so I could not allow an ailing car to get in the way. When I finally made it to work, I vowed it would be the last day I drove that car. I had bought the car as a rebuilt salvage four years earlier while living in Georgia, and from the inception there were problems. Most annoying was the issue of the key being stuck in the ignition because the gear knob wouldn't release—apparently, a defect with 2001 Volvo cars. It took two years for us to figure out how to solve that problem. Then, the air conditioning system broke, and I couldn't afford to repair it as I had spent all my cash to purchase the car. So, in the summers, I packed Ziploc bags with ice and carried a gallon of water in the car to cool down. I didn't care about the absentee car radio; silence was good. I was more concerned about the uncontrollable vibration anytime I accelerated above 60 miles per hour. But I was grateful. At least I had a car that had conveyed me around the Peach State, a car that still cranked out enough juice to make it to Florida and sustain me here for a year.

My boss suggested it was probably time to stop putting money into an old car. He had already seen my front bumper guard grating along the office's parking lot and had recommended an auto body shop that could fix the bumper. Now, an engine problem?

Not having worked long enough to save for a car, I took the dive and financed a 2007 MINI Cooper despite my aversion to debt. The car was a red and white version of the gold, two-door MINI with white bonnet stripes and white hard top plastered on my vision board. The MINI felt like home. Something about sitting low in a fast, Mr. Bean-inspired car was beyond satisfying. Though I never was a car aficionado, the boost of this turbo go kart changed the game. I was in love!

Serendipitously, I noticed more MINIs on the road, and each time I broke into a silly, girlish smile. I was part of the MINI community—a set of drivers who mutually identified by honking as we passed one another. I still don't understand how it happened, but I appreciated the synchrony that prompted us to find our MINI mates side-by-side on highways and in open parking spaces.

My brother Greg and I spoke almost daily. He heard the excitement in my voice.

"Girl, yuh still giddy?" He probed, clearly amused.

I was, indeed. The job, the car, the comfort of Florida's perpetual heat had all done it for me.

The late Bahamian preacher Dr. Myles Munroe taught that if we believe a thing, we must plan for that thing. The vision board plastered on my bedroom wall illustrated my plan, and it was becoming a living reality. It held colored photos of my breakout book *They Taught Me To Think*; a gold and white MINI Cooper; sampling of US currency to represent increased finances; an image of an entrepreneur working on a laptop beachside, indicative of the mobile lifestyle I desired; the caption of "Your faith has healed you" for my physical healing; flags and names of countries I wanted to visit; a callout to take the message of God's goodness globally; and a Mediterranean-styled ranch house.

Upon seeing this vision board, a visiting friend chuckled, "Wow, you're like a kid with your pictures!" I *was* like a child, and I loved it! For the in-your-face presence of this board reminded me daily of my goals, my reason for being. It was a constant reminder to trust my Father in heaven to make it happen. The anticipation of it all was exciting.

I had come from dark days of depression in Georgia. I still remembered what it was like to live outside of one's purpose, and I would not wish that misery on anyone. Now, a new day had dawned, and I unapologetically enjoyed every split second of it. So if childlike images on a wall helped me stay focused on the prize, the end would justify those means.

Chapter Two

A Better Me

Doubtless, I am a better writer than speaker. Writing allows me time to deliberate, to organize my thoughts, and to edit for effective communication. Since my freshman year of high school, I've been uncomfortable with public speaking for the same reasons many people are—feeling nervous about facing an audience, stumbling from one point to the next, feeding questions. Of course, the irony of having worked most of my career in a profession that requires public speech does not escape me. Yet for the more than fifteen years of my teaching, each time before stepping into the classroom I psyched myself as though preparing for battle. While I loathed teaching, I reminded myself that after college this was the only related job I could find. In the early teaching days, my effervescent personality served well in concealing my uneasiness about classroom duties. I was sufficiently articulate, witty, and beaming with the optimism of a professional woman in her early thirties as I mimicked the style of my favorite mentor-teacher. It worked, as students jostled to enroll in my classes. But as I aged, sustaining the facade became difficult. I was a fraud in front of the class, a hypocrite, a defector of my true self. For I knew without a doubt that while I struggled to speak publicly, I waxed most comfortably on a page. This was where I felt at home. It was my niche. To know me was, and still is, to read my words.

Such self-knowledge is important to becoming a better person. It entails knowing one's strengths and the threats to those strengths, being aware of personal weaknesses and perceiving the opportunities to correct those shortfalls. For me, this idea of Strengths, Weaknesses, Opportunities, and Threats (SWOT) was not just a business theory I learned in school; it was a tool for personal rebranding. Having paid attention to who I am over the years, I know my strengths to be congeniality, self-control, and faith. My glaring weaknesses include impatience and inability to multitask.

In my quest for self-improvement, each day was an opportunity to grow in character and be true to the person I was created to be. Unabashedly woman, I was strong, vulnerable, and ever dependent on my Lover and Lord. I built this platform of self-understanding by studying the things I loved and acknowledging those I didn't. In so doing, I recognized the need for synergy—that captivating consequence of two or more entities working in unison. For me, synergy was not just a pretty, rhythmic word. Even greater was its power to inspire.

My desire for synergy stemmed from admiring favorite living music legends like Barbra Streisand. I recalled a live performance of "Somewhere" by Streisand and Il Divo where Streisand's perfect pace and diction showed off her ageless appeal. The maturity and power with which she delivered each note gave me goose bumps. Similar responses were evoked from famous duets like those by Andrea Bocelli and Sarah Brightman; Celine Dion and Josh Groban; Celine and Peabo Bryson; Peabo Bryson and Regina Belle. And who of my generation could resist the harmonious, classic rendition of "Endless Love" by Diana Ross and Lionel Richie? The gorgeous, toothy Ms. Ross remains an elegant star whose showmanship rivals her dazzling vocals and whose on-stage poise still unhinges audiences worldwide.

Yet my all-time synergistic duo has to be the commanding, mesmerizing matchup of master sopranos Kathleen Battle and Jessye Norman in "Spirituals in Concert," backed by a full choir and orchestra. Glorious perfection! I hold my breath on almost every note, breathing and blinking only between notes, lest I miss some riveting detail. The coupling of these artists' exquisite vocal charm sets up the undeniable synergy. And I feel so much better for it—even to the point of belting out my own disastrous rendition.

Surely, there is no substitute for quality voices effortlessly mounting notes in sweet synchrony. Such evocations exist with equally powerful quartets, orchestras, choirs, collaborations, and musicals. Especially rich are those that integrate genres, like those melding song with dance, drama, etc.

I marvel too at the gastronomic delights of designers like Massimo Bottura—great chefs who step beyond the kitchen garden and produce magnificently mind-altering creations. I'm inspired by the art and science of good cooking (and eating, of course) because of its ability to challenge culinary artists to reimagine and repurpose shapes, colors, textures, and flavors that diminish boundaries. It urges me to engage with the world broadly, boldly. The attention to detail inspires me to be attentive to my craft; to touch people and make their lives brighter for a moment—hopefully for a lifetime.

This is the power of synergy! It moves us to be our best. It exposes the unlimited magnitude of human capabilities and inspires in all of us excellence to be stunning at what we were born to do.

Chapter Three

Limp

When the end of 2015 came, I acquired health insurance through my job and was finally under doctors' care. Between moving from Georgia and changing jobs in Florida, it had been more than a year since my lumpectomy. Because no immediate follow-up treatment of chemotherapy or radiation was done, the stage III breast cancer had metastasized to my bones. Cliché intended, there was nothing much medical science could do. My oncologist's best advice was to make my remaining days as comfortable as possible. I wasn't worried—concerned, but not worried. God knew this was not the life I had planned. I understood that the solution was out of the doctors' hands. But I also knew God could fix this. Only He could perform the healing miracle I needed and sought.

Amidst this assumption of my being a walking dead, I had a nagging sense that it was not over—that my life was not over, so I should not give up. That nagging kept me laser focused on the two people who had the power to improve my situation, God and me. In an odd, paradoxical way, I also felt there was no need to keep fighting. Time for fighting was over. It was now time to recline and experience the victory God had made available to me. Sometimes we fight, for we have to fight. Other times, we need to step aside and let God fight on our behalf—make room for God to show His brawn. The secret is knowing which strategy to engage at what time. Keeping one's ears close to God's lips is the only way to know what to do and when.

So I pressed in closer to hear God's voice. I hardly spoke; I listened more. Rather than think about the aggression of the disease and its capabilities, I saturated my mind with the many testimonies of God's miraculous healing recorded in the Bible and lived out in people I knew. I remembered the amazing recoveries of Lois Francois[1] and Mary Ann Kaiser[2], both friends of mine whom God healed of incurable diseases. These women are alive today and actively expanding the kingdom of God here in the United States and beyond. I was encouraged by these ladies who overcame so much. My suffering was nothing compared to theirs.

Nonetheless, my days were punctuated by excruciating pain as the disease had affected my left hip bone. While at work, I sat quietly at my desk and rocked out to Pandora music that streamed through my earphones. The music was a refreshing comfort to help me pass the day. After

---

[1] Lois Francois. *I Serve You the Back of Jesus.* (Bloomington, IN: WestBow Press, 2015).

[2] Mary Ann Kaiser. *Love That Heals: Let My Life's Love Song Sing to You.* (Lake Mary, FL: Creation House, 2013).

hours of editing, I needed a bathroom break. Pushing back my chair, I leaned forward to stand but could not move my left hip.

"God, please help," I whispered inaudibly through the pain.

I slid back in the chair and tried again cautiously. Slowly, I made it out of my seat and cubicle, holding on to the walls for support and praying in my mind for strength to make it to the bathroom without wetting myself. My boss saw me shuffling along the hallway. His puzzled stare said it all. Before he even spoke, I brushed him off good-naturedly.

"No worries, Boss. Just a little hip pain."

My smile set him at ease. I was trying to be brave and didn't want to seem like a drama queen. I'd never told him of my medical condition, although it was disclosed in my Human Resources file. He would hear it from my lips only if absolutely necessary. I made it to and from the bathroom uneventfully but notably aware of the increasing pain in my hip.

One subsequent day while reviewing promotional material for a then soon-to-be-published textbook on cell biology, content on the regenerative properties of cells caught my attention. The authors, who develop medicines and technology to aid cell rebuilding, reminded me that cells are living organisms that thrive or die under specific conditions. The information renewed my hope and refocused my prayers. Rather than pray in a general way for healing, I began to instruct the diseased bones, cells, and DNA in my body to heal, to repair. I engaged the creationist principles of think, speak, and create (TSC) to redirect the cellular rebuilding of my body. I spoke through the piercing pain in my hip, focusing on the life-giving outcome. With every shuffle and limp, I gave life to my body and thanked God for His authority and healing. There were bad days and good nights thereafter, but nothing deterred me. I was continuing to vie for my life first and for those of others who might believe as a result of this testimony. I would model faith so others could see and believe in the God who creates and restores life; in the God who is active, alive, and relevant; in the God who cares deeply about His offspring.

The pain in my body continued as the prescribed oxycodone every six to eight hours was not cutting it. I was going through two tablets every two hours, ten to twelve in a day, and they still weren't bringing relief. The pain was so much that I willingly limped into a medical supply store and purchased a walking cane to help me get around. It was a good thing I was alone in Florida because my use of the cane among my peeps in Georgia or New York would have been material for way too many jokes.

During this time, my oncologist tried various drugs to control the increasing cancer markers (indicators of the presence of cancer) in my body. Though the left hip bone was most affected, there was evidence of cancer scattered among bones in my back, shoulder, and right femur. The months of using tamoxifen treatment were unsuccessful as the markers still escalated. At that point, it was too late for traditional chemotherapy. So we continued trying other hormonal chemotherapy drugs that, according to progressive medical research, could produce better results without adverse side effects. After months of trial, the combination of faslodex and ibrance (drugs used to block estrogen and thus inhibit the cancer) plus monthly doses of xgeva (to treat the bones) worked. The cancer markers were slowly decreasing. I was finally able to exchange the clunky walking cane for a less-obvious pain reliever—a fentanyl patch pasted above my left breast.

Chapter Four

Finding Faith

An unsettling reality in our culture is the extent to which many people have lost confidence in governments, systems, and corporations. The old model of corporate and employee loyalty is long gone. Now, it's every man for himself. Even in industries that seemed insulated, it was only a matter of time before those fields and skilled personnel were disposed of. One of my former bosses is a statistic of this phenomenon of American economic culture. An IT professional, this gentleman has gone through about three layoffs in five years. And he is no slouch; he is a model manager. He, like so many others, is exasperated by companies that increasingly perpetuate such frustration.

But within this heartless system of corporate abuse, greed, and selfishness is a presence of the hearty God who patiently waits for us humans to access Him. I had long become a follower of this God and knew that to make Him and me happy I must have faith. Courage to believe and to take action as a result of that belief defines faith. It is staking everything on that belief. The Bible's countless examples of faith indicate how critical this concept is, for "without faith, it is impossible to please God" (Hebrews 11:6, NIV).

To boost my faith, I returned to one of my favorite examples of faith: the biblical report of a woman who had a chronic bleeding problem for twelve years. This woman had seen countless doctors who exploited her for money and left her worse off. After hearing about Jesus, she did not wait for a suggestion to seek healing. She had a need and hungrily pursued the One who alone could solve her medical problem. Jostling the crowd, she managed to touch a piece of Jesus's robe. Her efforts were enough. Her flow of blood dried up immediately! Simultaneously, Jesus felt energy leave Him and inquired about who had touched His robe. The woman eventually confessed and told her story. Impressed by her belief that prompted her desperate efforts, Jesus said to the woman, "'Daughter, you took a risk of faith, and now you're healed and whole. Live well, live blessed! Be healed of your plague'" (Mark 5:34, The Message).

I am not a theologian, but perfunctory reading of Scripture reveals equally dramatic records of God's miracle-working power:

- Jesus commanded a paraplegic man to walk. And the man walked! (Matthew 9:1-8; Mark 2:1-12; Luke 5:18-26).
- Jesus told a man with a withered hand to stretch it out. When the man obeyed, his hand grew into

normalcy (Matthew 12:10-13; Mark 3:1-7; Luke 6:6-11).

In seeking solutions for my life, I didn't need heavy theology or exegetical posturing. I needed measurable evidence of God's power. Jesus delivered those results. He did not just engage in intellectual discussions. He embodied intellect, power, and deliverables. And He changed lives.

I wanted to see such change personally. I longed to see the impossible shattered, not just to improve my quality of life, but also to showcase the fascinating Deity whose awesomeness melts my heart and the hearts of so many of His objects of affection worldwide. I desired to show off God's relevance in our hedonistic, unbelieving world.

At the same time, I had seen so often the incongruity of "believers" who didn't believe—Christians who routinely put more confidence in their doctor's diagnosis than in the Great Physician's. With the precision of a seasoned medical professional, these church-going experts recited the physiology and pharmacology of their medical conditions. Yet they hesitated, and in some cases refused, to exercise the same confidence in God's ability to change their circumstances, to heal them. I was saddened by such faithlessness and timidity. I wanted to encourage believers and non-believers to trust God, to give opportunities for God to demonstrate His unmatched skills in their situations. I wanted to be a poster girl for God's amazing power. Why not? I was poised for the miracle. I believed and was hungry for it.

Therefore, I continued thanking God daily for healthy cell regeneration—understanding the reality of my physical condition and at the same time being intimately acquainted with the miraculous power of the Creator, the One who continues to speak life through His creation. This conviction that propelled me was not an occasional exercise of faith, but an active faith that became my triumph.

Living on the edge daily with God increased our intimacy. I listened to Him 24/7, getting used to the sound and sense of His voice. I carefully chose my surroundings, sidestepping negativism as much as possible. I did only the things that moved me forward and upward, avoiding and/or discontinuing unfruitful relationships.

Intimacy is often borne from suffering. Whether spouses, lovers, or friends, suffering together intensifies relationships. For those of us in love relationships, we want to know that our lovers are with us because they have given up something valuable to be with us. We feel special because of their sacrifice. And they feel equally prized to know that we have surrendered good things in choosing them. Is there a love relationship flakier than the one untested?

Intimacy also has its privileges. Therefore, I expect unique blessings from God because of our relationship. We love each other. We trust each other. Other people's lack of faith or reluctance to believe God has nothing to do with me. I build relationship with God, and He responds with results. I subscribe to a long line of Bible heroes—Noah, Moses, Abraham, Sarah, Rahab,

David, etc.—who believed God and were phenomenally rewarded for their faith and righteousness.

Of course, while building this faith platform, I was acutely aware of the possibility of falling flat and not experiencing the miracle I needed—of being a mocking stock. But faith concerns itself not with negative thinking. Faith focuses on the positive, amidst incredible odds.

And faith is not limited to the religious community. Fans of USA professional sports recall the thrilling victory of the 2016 NBA's Cleveland Cavaliers over the Golden State Warriors after trailing 3-1 in the series. During the same year in Major League Baseball, the Chicago Cubs defeated the Cleveland Indians and overcame a century-long drought in winning the World Series. Then, at the 2017 NFL Super Bowl, the New England Patriots electrifyingly trounced the Atlanta Falcons in a game that secured Tom Brady's place as the top-shelf quarterback of all time.

The common thread in each of these victorious teams was the ability to come from behind and overcome seemingly insurmountable odds. Such tenacity is built into the human DNA. We humans are extensions of the Creator who infused astounding life into nothingness. The result is undeniable—that the seemingly impossible becomes tangible when we envision possibility and toil to make it happen.

Chapter Five

The American Dream

Rooted into the quest for betterment in the United States is a ludicrous notion that one has to go into debt to achieve the American Dream. The USA is one of those places where fabulously extraordinary things happen. It's where hard-working, ordinary people have a fair chance to save money and secure a peaceful future for them and their families with minimal government interference. It's the place where today's fast-food flipper becomes tomorrow's six-figure earner simply by studying prudently and landing a job in a high-demand field. It's where a single mother struggles to raise her son, who later wins a professional sports contract with millions in earnings. This is the greatness of America! Almost overnight the pauper can become a prince. Thus, millions of people transnationally board planes, boats, rafts, trucks, etc., for a gamble at this magical land that makes such dreams happen. Unfortunately, for too many, the magic is only an illusion.

To some extent, I was one of those deluded dreamers. I had come to America and done the education thing to secure my future success. Rather than pot of gold, I ended with a vat of debt that has yet to translate into valuable return on investment. Was that worth it? Absolutely not! Most of what I gained in racking up student debt could have been acquired from a disciplined approach to self-learning.

This ensnaring illusion was evident not just in my life but also in so many others, immigrants and non-immigrants alike, who spend the first quadrant of their lives pursuing a pricey dream then awakening to a hideous reality. Suffocating with debt from their massive, empty houses and lifestyles, they had no choice but to slave daily on jobs they dread just to maintain a façade of success. Where is the pleasure in this? What is its quality of life?

Years ago, I was on a cruise to Labadee, Haiti, as I celebrated my fortieth birthday with friends. It was my first cruise, and I was excited. I had flown from Missouri to Miami, where we boarded the cruise. From the time we reached the Caribbean shore, I was uninterested in ziplining, snorkeling, kayaking, or whatever else Royal Caribbean was offering. My girls and I were happy just to sit under the sun and gaze at the tranquil waters—tall, icy fruit drinks in both hands. Aside from local vendors selling handcrafts, there weren't bells and whistles on that Haitian peninsula, but its peace and comfort were unmatched. Occasionally, I got up and stood hip-deep in the warm ocean water. It was a throwback to that little girl who frolicked in the waters of Guyana. I wished I could stay in Labadee longer as the weight of the US lifted.

Almost ten years later I cannot shake the airy, stress-free feeling of that Caribbean paradise. It was a reminder of a simpler time and place. The time of my parents and fore-parents, a time when working 8 to 4 and returning home to good food, light chores, and siesta were more than enough. A world where food, clothing, shelter, and much laughter were all the luxury anybody needed. A debt-free existence where people competed wit against wit. It wasn't about who had the best house, car, bank account, etc. Life in those days was only about being and giving.

Maybe mine's a post-midlife nostalgia. But in these more recent days, I have realized that my parents never owned a credit card or carried around debt. They saved always and purchased nonessentials only when they could afford them. Everything they have they own; nothing is borrowed. In early adulthood in New York, I thought them outdated and uninformed about American culture. Were I not so pseudo-sophisticated, I would have followed their lead sooner and avoided unnecessary financial pitfalls.

Clearly, I was anxious about my school loans and other lesser debts. I had cashed out my retirement accounts and was eking by on disability insurance after being laid off from the dreamy copyediting job with the international publisher in South Florida. To be out of work yet again was amusing rather than frustrating. I could no longer take this seriously. The company had been forced to downsize because of loss of revenue. My boss and his entire team of copywriters and copyeditor were among the hundred employees displaced.

Today's corporate job search was not unlike online dating. A candidate has a need, so she scouts the relevant sites. She finds a match, makes connection, and the wooing begins. (Hopefully, she has done her homework about the suitor and likes what she sees.) After weeks or months of distanced communication, it's time to meet face to face—only to discover it was all a ruse. But she had already envisioned her new life and was too emotionally invested. She wasted time and energy and got played! Perhaps only a simpleton could keep putting herself out there like that.

Recurring themes in my work history duly noted, I decided not to pursue another job opportunity, for I had neither the physical nor emotional stamina to do so. Instead, I would sit back and do what God required of me. I would write to celebrate Him. Sure, I needed money to sustain myself and eliminate my debts. The disability insurance kept me barely afloat, and I didn't see how I could possibly eliminate my debts without income. Somehow, I had to dig deep and entrust that need to God. All my human efforts to self-provide had failed miserably, and God was teaching me to trust Him for my everyday and future needs. Each time I had tried to do the normal, commonsensical thing it had ended badly. God obviously had a different method in mind for my need provision.

So I set my goals, though I had no idea how they

would be reached. I amended my vision board, revisited it often, affirmed and believed that everything listed on it would be realized. The logistics of this plan to acquire certain finances, work remotely, live simply, etc. were nonexistent. But that didn't stop me from planning and projecting into a fabulous future. I was quietly trusting God to fulfill these plans while learning to relinquish my own anxiety.

Through all this, Mommy hinted at my returning to Georgia to live with the family, where I wouldn't have to be concerned about paying for rent, food, and other living expenses. For the thirty-plus years we lived in the US, Mommy never quite came around to the idea of having her unmarried children live away from the family home. She tolerated it but didn't prefer it. So, this was the perfect opportunity for her to play that card, and her suggestion made financial sense. But anybody who knows me could have perceived the unlikelihood of my following that proposition. Georgia? Heavens, no! Not again. I had taken a colossal beatdown in Georgia and would have to be a masochist to return there to live.

During my private, internal revolt against the Peach State, I was also quietly aware that if God tapped me at any point to return to Georgia, I would do His bidding. I had been around long enough to know that God could actually do that. I had also been through enough to know that when God speaks I would humble myself and submit to Him regardless of my inclinations. Disobeying God was always foolish.

In the meantime, living in Florida was right for me.

It offered the tranquility and freedom I craved, but these did not come easily. Yes, I knew of my family's love and their desire to help solve my problems, but this pursuit between God and me was more personal. Sometimes, family, though well-meaning, were prone to getting in the way of God's pruning, and I couldn't afford that interference. God and I would become much better acquainted through this saga.

Fortunately, I had obeyed God and published Part One of my story. The release of the book gave me credibility and silenced the naysayers. My family and friends finally heard my voice and took me seriously. Most gave actual feedback that celebrated the accomplishment. Others quietly supported by purchasing books. This was sufficient validation.

How did I not realize this was all it took to earn some respect among my family and peers? Simply doing what I said I would do for many years. It's true; talk really is cheap. People want results. They want to see what we can do and identify with our experiences. They want to see themselves in us—the good, bad, and ugly. Any idiot can talk at length. But it takes discipline, strength, and knowledge to produce something that adds value to people's lives.

No doubt, the earlier release of part one of this book enhanced my family relations. My brother Roger and I spoke every Sunday afternoon just before his weekly phone marathon with Mommy. He checked in to make sure I was afloat medically, financially, and emotionally. We got caught up on the family, politics, church news, his latest world travels, and miscellaneous items. We looked forward to this phone time together during which I pleaded for him to hook me up romantically with one of his many delicious buddies. His response was always the same:

"They don't want youuuu!" His lengthened *you* was intended to indicate derision.

"Ahhh, you iz a was'e a time! I gon find me own man," I railed.

We'd chuckle at the slim possibility of that happening and move on until a later conversation when I would playfully mess with him again about being a blocker, a hindrance to my love life.

What an uncanny twist in December 2016 when Roger was taken suddenly after a supposedly low-risk heart surgery. His death, though gut-wrenching, created for me an unexpected benefaction. I was able to accomplish a few more goals on my vision board, and this increased my faith to help me attain the others.

Indeed, God had been watching over me all along and had condensed the time as He promised many years before through the prophecy. He rescued me and secured a modest future for me. All through the seesawing job situations, relocations, health crises, etc., God providentially had my back. And He had been using the good and the unflattering moments of my life to teach me that my success would be achieved not by the norms of traditional education but by learning to think differently.

Chapter Six

An Allegory

Thus, by self-assignment, I am the king's servant. Child of the king by birth, servant of the king by choice. Those close to me know of my obsession with the king, sometimes to the point of irritation. Theirs, not mine. So, why my fixation with him?

Daddy and I have had a special bond since childhood. I was a sickly child who often missed school, and it was he who managed my health. Almost every month during my preadolescent years, he'd traipse me to the doctor to treat some malady of mine—asthma, measles, asthma, worm infection, asthma again. In those days in Guyana, we knew nothing of asthma inhalers, so every one of my bouts had to be treated by a doctor. Daddy's job offered the type of flexibility to make those emergency trips. As public health inspector, his tasks ranged from inspecting meat at the local abattoir and butcher shops to inspecting international cargo ships that docked in Georgetown. On the days when he did double duty by taking me to the doctor then checking in on the docks, I looked forward to scoring tasty foreign candies or sweet biscuits (cookies) from the ship's crew. I didn't mind being sick on those days. I was touring the city with Daddy while my sister Diane was stuck in a classroom.

Since those days, I quietly identified as Daddy's girl. Though I never heard my siblings assign the term to me nor has either of my parents affirmed this, I came to know I am that girl. Not that my sisters Heather and Diane weren't prized by Daddy, but I felt a special connection to him probably by virtue of my health-related vulnerabilities and the time he and I spent together.

Throughout the years into my adulthood, Daddy and I grew closer. Now that we live one state apart—he in Georgia and I in Florida—he looks forward to my frequent visits, for then he gets a chance to be pampered royally by his servant-daughter. This is his time to retire from assisting mommy in the kitchen and instead have me massage his feet and tuck him under a blanket as he reclines in front of the television. Or he can lounge in bed until afternoon and have his meals served whenever and wherever he wishes. If it's warm enough outside, we dine on the deck overlooking the vast kitchen garden that he and my brother Greg manage. There, the crew (Daddy, Mommy, Greg, and I) cackles heartily over meals while Daddy shows off their handiwork of okra, tomatoes, callaloo, eggplant, beans, lemongrass, peppers, squash, and herbs. While I despise Georgia because of the grave suffering it brought to my life, I cherish my time with the family.

I especially enjoy Daddy because he is a man of faith, not in some over-churched, unproductive way. His is the kind that pleases. One of my favorite recollections is of him buying his first car. He tells me that early in his career he had to travel from his hometown in the countryside into the capital city of Georgetown to do business. While waiting for the bus to take him home, he wandered into a nearby auto garage (car dealership) to kill time. A few hours later, neither license nor driving experience in hand, Daddy had set off on the forty-mile, maiden drive home and became one of the first car owners in his village—a local hero.

Through this and so many of his narratives, I see in him courage, faith, possibilities. He tells me the same stories every time, so I know how they all begin, progress, and end. I do not interrupt but engage with rapt attention as though hearing them all for the first time. Mommy and Greg don't understand how I tolerate the repetition, considering my renowned impatience. Obviously, my time with Daddy is less about the stories. At the same time, I learn something new as occasionally my 92-year-old father remembers tiny details about a story—details he hadn't mentioned before, details that enhanced the delivery and moral of his story.

Still, Daddy is only one part of an increasingly impressive parental team, each member worthy of a crown. But if ever I were to buy crowns to celebrate my parents (which I have secretly considered), I could see Mommy revolting:

"Girl, tek that stupid thing off meh head! You don' have work to do?"

With Mommy, it's always about the work. Daddy,

meanwhile, would wear his crown proudly, gleefully. Then, he and I would seal his coronation with a high-five—to the resignation of Mommy and Greg, who'd shake their heads and conveniently find somewhere else to be.

Epilogue

So, for the first time in my life I am ecstatic to the point of perpetual giddiness as I finally embody that perfect marriage of person and purpose. I live in my dream state and do daily what God designed me to do. I'm enjoying a remote lifestyle of writing to expand God's influence globally, and things are progressing well in my body. Through regular treatments and God's aggressive work, the cancer markers continue to decrease. While I still take oxycodone when needed to manage pain, I no longer require fentanyl as the excruciating hip pain is controlled. I will stay the course of treatment until this healing is empirically documented.

Obviously, death is unavoidable. At some point in the distant future, I will take my last bow and make room for the next act. Until such inevitable time, I live fiercely and fearlessly for God above.

Stay Connected

- Bookmark our website at http://theytaught
  metothink.com.
- Join our Facebook page to be informed of related
  events and updates.

Printed in the United States
By Bookmasters